CONTENTS

INTRODUCTION

HOW THE FINANCIAL GAME WORKS

#1 - MESSY BETTY & UNTIDY TOM

#2 - BROKE BOB

#3 - TIMMY TOO MANY

THE FINAL

Introduction

Have you ever wondered why, financially, things just seem a little off? Your portfolio *looks* correct. The advisor *sounds* good. Your accounts? Well, they *appear* to be sound and not losing too much money. If all is well, then what's the issue? That's a great question! Everything may look, sound and appear to be good on the outside, but is it really? Are you fully aware of your complete financial status? Just because the advisor says that it's so, doesn't mean that it's true. Additionally, just because something looks correct on the surface doesn't mean that it's sound underneath, take a closer look, you might just be surprised.

In this book, *Financially Speaking*, the author points out a few key concepts of what to look for in determining your true financial status. The book will also encourage you to become an educated investor and financial consumer. Many people don't have fifty, sixty or seventy more years to accumulate wealth again; once it's gone, it's gone. Do yourself a favor and read this book. In this book, you'll learn how to act instead of react. You'll also learn how to establish, maintain and continue your sound financial future for not only today but for the days to come. Read the book, you'll be glad that you did!

How the Financial Game Works

As it pertains to the financial arena, the game is certainly fixed. For those who understand the game and understand it well, they will be the victors. The word *game* denotes a competitive activity involving skill, chance, or endurance on the part of two or more persons who play according to a set of rules. To achieve a surmountable level of excellence and financial aptitude within the industry, one must be financially educated and astute, to say the least. Becoming financially educated does not mean that one must matriculate at a local university; rather, one must be willing to learn through personal research and discovery. Once thoroughly researched and discovered, one must then execute. Just as in life, it's all a game and whoever calculates, strategizes and executes the best will receive the best. Note to self, the odds are in your favor. What's next? The dice are in your hands, now run the table. You got this!

MESSY BETTY & UNTIDY TOM

They mess up often...and it's at your expense.

The first thing that I want to let you know about FA's is that they are so prone to mess up that it's not even funny. Some FA's mess up on a regular basis, simply put, they don't know what the heck they are doing. Besides suggesting the obvious, what I do wish to tell you is how you should effectively manage such facades when encountered. Today, I wish to propose to you what it is that you should look for, listen for and feel like when an FA is messing you over.

One may ask, "What should I *look* for if I think that an FA is messing me over?" The first thing that you want to look for is mistakes. Mistakes can appear in many different ways. Mistakes come in all sizes, shapes and forms (literally *forms*, but I'll get to that a little later). Never mind, let's get into *forms* right now (pay close attention). Here we go....

Forms. Paperwork. Documents. Some FA's have absolutely no clue as to how to complete basic fundamental account opening paperwork. In one company that I worked for, often times, an FA would call in upset because a client's account had been closed. Why was the account closed? The account had been closed because for the previous sixty to ninety days preceding the account closure, we had been asking for the proper paperwork to be submitted and we had yet to receive it. During this time, the FA just continued to over look our multiple requests. Ninety days later, they've now received a deposit from a client that must be deposited; however, the funds cannot be deposited because the account is now closed.

And oh my, the FA dare not go back to the client advising that the account has been closed due to a user-error; failure to pay attention to a weekly notification. Side bar, I'll give you a little background as to how this whole "paperwork" thing works.

Okay, say for instance you are the FA and you have a client that you wish to open an account for. You have worked so long and so hard to gain this client's confidence and business that it has now paid off an entire two years later. Finally, the client due to your persistence, professionalism and dogged determination, has caved. You now have the business. You, the FA, was able to pull this *busy* client into your office to complete new account opening paperwork (woo-hoo!) and you are very excited. You're thinking, "I am finally about to seal the deal with his John Hancock. I did an excellent job! See, persistence and hard work *does* pay off!" You're mentally patting yourself on the back. You are giving yourself an imaginary high-five! Look, you are on your way. Oh, not to mention, this is a big book of business. Meaning, this account is worth $10M plus. You are *doing it*!

So, the client's in your office, you're talking about this, conversing about that...not giving any attention to the paperwork at all. You are just very excited to have sealed the deal. You give the completed paperwork a once over, everything looks good. You think, "We're good to go!" And hey, you may even give the completed paperwork yet another quick gander just for good measure (you know, to make yourself look competent in front of the client). You decide, all looks well, it's a go. You and the client shake hands. You congratulate him on yet another great business deal and they're out the door. Boom, you're done!

The following morning, you give the paperwork to your assistant to scan into the new accounts database for processing. The assistant doesn't pay any attention to the paperwork because after all, she's new. She just got hired on and surely, you as the FA know what you are doing so why should she check behind her boss? No need, right? Papers are scanned in, papers are rejected, notification is sent *and* received but no reply is given. All is ignored. After all, your confidence as an FA is at an all-time high after just signing a $10M account to your firm, it's time to move out, ride the high and go get more business. By demonstration, the FA thinks, "Pay attention to notifications, *for what*?"

So, time comes and time goes. Notifications come, notifications go. Red flags come, red flags go. Still, no action on behalf of the FA. Until, the client decides that they now wish to make a sizable deposit into his account for a specific transaction. The deposit is for his beloved only daughter who is presently flying out to France as we speak, this deposit must go through (with this client, it's not optional but mandatory). The FA is excited about the deposit and attempts to deposit the funds into the account. However, the FA soon discovers to his dismay that the account has been red-flagged for ninety days and closed for sixty. The FA now thinks, "Oh my! Whatever shall we do with this deposit?

There is a red flag on this account." Again, this account has been requiring the proper paperwork since the first week of its opening but the FA failed to respond to the notification. This is how FA's get into sticky situations, and by "sticky" I mean unethical situations. I cannot even begin to tell you the things that I have heard and witnessed because an FA failed to reply to a notification and now they sit in a bit of a quandary wondering what to do. Personally, I have been privy to situations, whereby, an FA has placed themselves under such duress and let me tell you, it's not pretty as one might imagine. When an FA is under distress, they will do almost *anything,* up to and including illegal acts at times. Why do you think some Financial Advisors end up in jail? Do an Internet search. You won't have to search long before a list populates. It's really not as uncommon as one might think, it's just not highly publicized but it happens.

Below is a list of asinine questions that were asked by FA's that were in distress:

- "Can't I just sign the client's name? I mean, they are out of the country and I can't bother them. It's just a signature; I mean, to bother the client for a basic signature is absurd!"
- "Can't you just open the account without the proper paperwork being on file? I'll get the proper paperwork to you, I promise. Just open the account, I don't want the client to know that I messed up. It took me so long to get this account. They're a judge, I don't want to look stupid, you know?"

- "We've sent in the proper identification for this client, what's the issue now? They're not a terrorist! Just remove the red flag and open the account please!" (Situation: Expired identification submitted as *valid* identification when it's not. Why? I'll give you one guess. Yelp, you're right...because it's expired. Now, why didn't our intelligent high-scoring-Series 7-exam-passing FA know this before they submitted the expired identification? Exactly, your guess is as good as mines. I have no clue!)
- "I can just change the name on the paperwork? I mean, it's only an "i" needing to be changed to an "e", I can do that right? I don't want to bother the client for this type of stuff, it just seems so remedial. This is a $50M account. I will not bother them for this."
- "Forget it! I'll just have someone at my branch remove the block. I don't need your assistance." (Situation: This is when and account has been closed and should remain closed but the branch wishes for it to be opened so that they can make a deposit. The account is closed for a reason. Fix the reason and the account can be legally re-opened per federal guidelines.)
- "I'll just scan a blank document into the new account opening system, have it reject out so that we can buy ourselves more time to get the proper account paperwork onto the system, can I do that?" (HUNH?!?!?!? You would like to do WHAT AGAIN?!?!?)

- "I need you to send me the K-1 tax document for the client? The client needs it, he is about to prepare his taxes." (411: The K-1 tax document is not issued by the investing firm to the client; rather, it's issued to the client by the corporation/partnership. The document goes straight to the client from the corporation/partnership, not from the investment firm to the client. The FA should know this information as this is a vital part of the role of an FA...know your business, know your people, know your processes and your paperwork, please.)
- "Can't I change the social security number on the application itself, initial the change for the client and then re-submit the paperwork for processing? I really don't want to have to bother the client again. I have gone back to them three times now already. I'm beginning to now look like I don't know what I am doing." (Thoughts: Quite possibly you don't know what you're doing, have you ever considered that? You may need to ask someone like your Complex Service Manager for assistance [and hopefully, they're not new and they know what they are doing]. Geesh!)
- "I know that the signature is missing but can't we just process the paperwork anyway? They told me that they wanted this account open and that they would complete the paperwork once they arrived back into the country." (Situation: In this case, the FA hasn't met the client at all. The FA knows nothing about the investment strategies or behaviors of the client. The

FA doesn't even know the client themselves; therefore, no signature no account, period. More than likely, this client came through a *referral*. This type of client is a major candidate for possible fraud and may quite possibly be an active member of the OFAC list [the OFAC list is a list of specially designated nationals and blocked persons that pose a potential threat to our system. You can read more about the OFAC list by visiting: www.treasury.gov])

- "Can't I just create the account password for the client? They gave me permission to do so. I know them. I've known them for years, it's okay. I'll set the password for them." (Thoughts: Uhm...noooo, this should not be done. How about we let the client set the password for the client? You can assist the client, but please, allow the client to engage in the process as this is their personal account and must be owned as such.)

So, you see, mistakes can be crucial when it comes to your FA. Your FA must be thorough and own up to their mistakes. Mistakes should be owned; even if it makes the FA look like an idiot and could prove to be quite costly, up to and including losing the account. In this field, integrity is key. If there's no integrity, there's no business. The New York Times Bestselling Author of *The 21 Irrefutable Laws of Leadership*, John Maxwell states, "Integrity is the quality most needed to succeed in business." Dr. John Maxwell knows about leadership and integrity very well. Dr. Maxwell is an internationally recognized leadership expert, speaker, coach, and author who has sold over 19 million books and he's a billionaire; so yeah, I would say, he definitely knows a *little* something about leadership and integrity.

Another speck for us to consider when wondering if you're being messed over by your FA is their presence. Is your FA present for you? Does your FA like to disappear while appearing that they really are present? Are they available to you? In this section, we will look into a few areas that may give us the answer to the afore-mentioned questions.

So, how can you know if your FA is playing games and disappearing on you? Simply put, your FA is hardly around but why? When an FA is predisposed to disappearing on you, typically, they'll have their assistant manage most details. An assistant is good and can manage some things but not all things. Remember, the fee scale is aligned with the Financial Advisor, not with the assistant. So, if your FA doesn't return your calls or text messages, if they are always skipping out and re-scheduling meetings and appointments with you; more than likely, they are intentionally avoiding you.

Now, there may be a good reason as to why they are not present and readily available; nonetheless, they aren't there. Chances are, there's generally a good reason so give them a chance to explain; however, listen and listen carefully. Ask questions; make them work for your business. If you feel like they are trying to feed you a bunch of mess; yelp, they probably are. Be professionally candid with the FA.

Re-affirm with your FA your expectations as their client and ask for their compliance. Be ready for the answer.

The FA may not be able to meet your demands and if that's the case, then you'd better start shopping around for a new FA as this one can no longer manage the relationship or your money successfully.

A good FA will be honest with you. They will let you know what is really going on and what the true issue is. It may be that the FA has grown exponentially and didn't plan well enough to properly manage the increase of client demands. Or, conceivably, maybe the FA has had a personal matter to escalate out of control and it's now spilling over into his professional life. Although the FA believes himself to be managing quite well, the truth of the matter is that he is not and it's showing rather clearly. I would suggest that you speak to your FA, give them a chance to explain. Again, if the FA doesn't come forward and advise with some general level of transparency, it may be time for a change. Remember, go with your gut feeling. I always like to give people a second, third and fourth chance in most situations. However, if you feel as though you have been patient enough and have afforded this FA every opportunity to change and yet they have not, I would suggest that you change. Why? Reason being, the flag has been raised. The FA is now aware that you feel that something is off center, and you do not want your financial portfolio to suffer because of it. Remain professional but change immediately.

Below are six indicators that your FA is not present (and again, they should be):

- S/he consistently misses your phone calls and/or text messages
- S/he regularly makes excuses to defend themselves against you and it's always for their benefit (but then again, isn't that how excuses work? To the advantage of the volunteer?)
- S/he steadily defers to the assistant, even when you've consistently requested for the FA not to
- As the client, you find yourself constantly repeating requests as though you've never asked; although, many times, you have
- S/he maintains a flippant attitude regarding your financial matters/requests
- Evidentiary disengagement; it's become quite clear that they are not fully engaged in the process with you or with your money

The list above are just a few indicatives, there may actually be additional signs that are telling of the fact that your FA is not present. Again, pay attention to your gut feeling, don't depend solely on what you see and hear. The words and actions of others may try to deceive but your gut feeling will never mislead you. Your gut is there to help you, so, pay attention and then respond accordingly.

What if things don't look right? You know, things just aren't adding up, what do you do? Great ask! When things aren't adding up or making sense and I can't put my finger on it but I'm still unsettled, I start digging. I start asking questions. I start aggressively researching. I refuse to give up or stop looking for what it is that I didn't know I would find.

Oft times, due to their extensive expertise, FA's really know how to cover things up; and quite well, might I add. Whether it's placing the blame on someone else or pretending to be unaware when they really are; an FA can cover up with the best of them. Unfortunately, the grand closeting of the FA, more times than not, arrives at the financial decrement of the client. In my experience as a financier, I have seen clients almost lose it all simply because they were afraid to do one thing...ask questions; frankly put, they were just too afraid to ask. Never, I repeat never, be afraid to ask questions. You don't know what you don't know but asking questions will definitely bring you one step closer to finding out what you *need* to know.

I remember a particular client who had failed to pay attention to his monthly financial statements. At the end of the year, when tax time rolled around, they were very surprised. Much to the client's dismay, the FA had moved their entire financial portfolio onto a managed platform without the consent of the client. What was so bad about the move? The move was bad because for starters, the client never gave their consent to initiate the transaction. Secondly, the FA never disclosed the fees for the move to the client. Therefore, the client was assessed fees for a platform move that they never consented to. Now let me say this, the platform change was actually disclosed within the monthly statement. However, the client wasn't versed on reading it, so each month the client just discarded the statement as a nonessential. One may ask, "Well, how was the issue discovered if no questions and no understanding was rendered by the client? How did the client find out?" Good question. The client discovered this atrocity by receiving a tax statement. Once reviewed, there were significant gains on certain positions that were successfully managed while on said platform. In the investment world, significant gains equal significant tax payments (unless your accountant is able to find a legal loophole for the gains, but that's a different book, different title.).

The client contacted me and was very upset and belligerent due to the recent discovery of increased gains, which in turn meant, increased taxes. One would think that the client would be happy about the gains, right? Wrong. The client was dismally flustered as they never provided consent for the platform move. The client just kept mumbling to themselves the entire time, "I thought something wasn't right, I just didn't know what." I felt really bad as the FA definitely breached the trust of the client. To the FA's credit, I have seen where the client just gave total autonomy to the FA in allowing the FA to do as they saw fit. Allowing someone to have total control over your money is very dangerous. Why would you trust someone that much and for no reason? I understand that the relationship between an FA and the client can be pretty close, like a marriage even. However, with that being said, no one should ever have total autonomy over your money but you. What if they lose your money? You are now 70 years old, can you *really* afford to start all over from the age of 70? For most, the answer is a resounding no.

So you see, we definitely want to ask questions and become educated through good sound information. Please make sure that you are reading your monthly statements. Be fully aware of your financial position as it pertains to your financial portfolio. Ask questions when needed, even ask questions when not needed. Just ask questions; that way, you'll get into the successful habit of asking.

Some clients have established trust funds for their grandchildren within their financial portfolios. Others may have chosen to set a variety of financial goals or may have financial instruments hidden within the portfolio itself. Wouldn't it be advantageous for you to ask a question or two regarding your portfolio, its performance along with its contents? Perhaps, you could review a statement or two? Here's a tip, if you're not too familiar with how to read your portfolio statement, no worries, you can always contact the service center directly and inquire of the rep on how to read your statement. In doing so, you're appearing to do two things: hiding your face while saving face. I say this because some clients do not relish the thought of appearing to not know something that they themselves know that they really should know. And I get it, I do. I mean, what person enjoys looking like an idiot, when they're really not? Personally, I do not enjoy appearing incompetent before any person, however, I'll endure the discomfort to gain the advantage, how about you? So, the workaround is to call around. Contact the phone service center directly, ask the client service rep to go over your statement with you and they will be more than happy to do so. If you feel that you have a new person on the line that isn't quite sure of what they are looking at, politely hang up and call back. It may seem rude but it really isn't. Notice that I said, "politely" disconnect the call and call back. Reason being, you are in the fifth grade and right now and you do not need a second grader trying to teach you fifth grade math. You need a sixth grader and above to teach you, someone who knows what they are talking about. You are already in the dark so there's no need to get shy now. You could also just ask for a more seasoned rep or you could even request a manager, it all just depends on the level of comfortability that you have with managing this particular scenario. There's a myriad of different ways in which you could acquire a more seasoned rep, I'll leave that up for you to decide; nonetheless, decide!

There's no feeling like the one you get when you know that you are talking to someone on the other end of the phone that actually knows what it is that they are talking about. Just think, the next time that you speak to your FA and have a specific question regarding the information that's reflected on your statement, you'll be impressive because you've now been educated and you know what you're talking about, what you're looking at and how to interpret most of the information that you see. Way to go! You're now educated! You know what you're talking about now and I say, good for you! Remember, the client service center is your friend so use them. Most call centers are open later than your FA's office so you can call and get educated right over the phone without your FA even knowing and that's an awesome accomplishment! No, really; you took the initiative to find out something that you once didn't know but now you do. You are now drenched in pure awesome sauce!

In giving further consideration as to what one should look for in a FA when being messed over, one should also listen as well as look. You may ask yourself, "What should I *listen* for if I think that an FA is messing me over?" Looking, observing with the naked eye is one thing; however, to listen through observation with the inner ear is yet another. Listening for indicators is an entirely different ball game.

One indicator that you want to listen for is if the FA says one thing yet does another. In not keeping their word, the FA tells you one thing now but performs something else at a later date; this is totally unacceptable. A person's word is quite indicative of their integrity level. Steven Covey wrote:

> If I try to use human influence strategies and tactics of how to get other people to do what I want, to work better, to be more motivated, to like me and each other –while my character is fundamentally flawed, marked by duplicity or insincerity—then, in the long run, I cannot be successful.

Covey connects the success of an individual to the condition of their character. Character is said to be faulty by the very existence of "duplicity or insincerity". If the FA fails to keep their word, that is definitely a character flaw for sure that's negatively impacting and inconveniencing you at will. You must investigate and inquire. Do not tolerate such behavior; in so doing, you put your financial status at serious risk.

Another item that you should listen for is confusion. Yes, I say *listen* because the state of confusion can also be heard as well as seen. Confusion is an unsureness, a doubt, an ignorance. If your FA is speaking to you in uncertain terms about something that he is unsure of; however, he is trying to pass it off as certainty, you need to check your FA on that.

There is nothing wrong with admitting that you do not know. What *is* wrong, however, is the assertive passing of ignorance with no attempt to recant, investigate, acknowledge or correct the issue at hand. Dr. Martin Luther King Jr. stated, "*Nothing in all the world is more dangerous than sincere ignorance and conscientious stupidity.*" And I must say, that I too, agree with Dr. King. Have you ever met someone, maybe a friend of a friend or perhaps a family member that could not be wrong? I mean, they are right *all* the time. These types of individuals will go to their grave believing that they are right when a thousand other people have conferred, agreed upon and even proven that they are wrong; they just refuse to believe the truth.

An ignorant person (not knowing) that refuses to change and self-correct is a person with whom you do not wish to be around. Moreover, better yet, this is that; this is that person that you do not want managing your financial endeavors. Why? Great question. This type of person will march full speed ahead, knowing nothing while risking all...at your expense. Of course, should something go seriously wrong, you could always fire them. Nonetheless, the question remains, will you be able to retrieve the level of wealth that you once had? Will you still be able to take advantage of said opportunities or have they all depreciated? These are all questions and more that one should give considerable thought to as one's financial independency may so feebly hinge upon this very consideration.

Robert Kiyosaki says, "*Financial freedom is available to those who learn about it and work for it.*" In other words, make your FA work for your business. However, make yourself work for your own financial freedom. Both of you need to stay working. You need to stay working so that you can remain financially free. The FA, however, will need to be managed as such that he/she continues to work for your business with the realization that your business *and you* can leave at any given time, with or without warning.

You must learn, grow and know while your FA does the same. If every one is learning and growing then you both will be in a better position to serve one another. You, on one hand, will know what the FA is talking about. You'll know what to expect in regards to returns, taxation etc. Simultaneously, the FA is now aware as to the level of your understanding while also realizing that they must produce and produce at an acceptable rate to retain you as their client. Your FA must clearly understand and know that it is not okay to take your money and so-call "manage your money" while losing your money...this is not okay. It is never okay for your FA to lose your money simply because they refuse to stay relevant, leverage financial opportunities and streamline communications and processes. An acceptable demand must be placed upon the FA in a professional way to encourage them to do their best for you and for your financial portfolio. Successfully managing another's financial status, portfolio and independence is extremely important and it must be communicated as such.

Lastly, another tenet to look for while listening to your FA is ownership. The lack of ownership from your FA is a key indicator that they are not acting fiscally responsible. If it sounds like your FA is always passing the buck and never accepting their role in a particular situation, nine times out of ten, they are. You are right. They *are* passing the buck and very loudly, might I add.

Henry Ward Beecher says, "*Hold yourself responsible for a higher standard than anybody expects of you. Never excuse yourself.*" One must never excuse the faultiness of their FA. Hold your FA accountable for all actions, words and behaviors; in so doing, you are also holding yourself accountable as well. Oprah says, "...from an early age I knew that I was responsible for myself, and I had to make good." Oprah is right. You are responsible for you as well as for your financial portfolio and status.

Oft too many times, I have seen clients just leave everything up to their Financial Advisor. You ask the client this and they say, "Oh, I don't know. My FA would know that." You ask the client that and again, they would say, "Oh, don't ask me such things, ask him" (meaning the FA). This type of pompous arrogant nonchalant ignorant type of attitude would make my skin crawl. Why? Reason being, the client would say such things as though they were speaking intelligently when the contrary was the true of it all.

"Feeling" out your FA is also a query that must be exacted. Such things as: gut feelings, hesitancy, nervousness and fear along with a certain type of sadness (typically depression) are all pointers that can help to guide you to the true position of your Financial Advisor as it pertains to you, their actions and your financial portfolio. We'll look into these a little closer to accurately determine the feel of such effects.

What is a "gut feeling"? A gut feeling is an emotion that arises in the bed of your stomach that communicates to your mind that something is wrong or even may be that something is right. At any rate, if you get a gut feeling that's telling you not to trust something in regards to your FA, believe it. Some also call this feeling an *intuition*. Whether it's intuition, a gut feeling or an instinct...it's all the same. It's a key indicator that something has gone awry or that maybe even something is right and not wrong at all. Regardless of its communication, typically, you act on what's been communicated through this emotion. Tamara Mellon, a British fashion designer says, "*Everything I do is just really my intuition, and every time I go against my intuition, it's a mistake. Even though I may sit down and analyze and intellectualize something on paper, if I go against my gut feeling, it's wrong.*"

I remember another well-known individual that told of a time when they use to work in a shoe store. One night, as she was closing, a man came into the store looking really suspicious. Her first inclination was to leave the store. Her gut feeling told her to run but she didn't adhere to her intuition. She said to herself, "What if I look stupid and there's nothing wrong?" So she stayed. Unfortunately, the story didn't turn out so well for her. The incident became an unfortunate recall that forever marks her until this day. In retrospect, she stated that, "If I would have only obeyed my first instinct, that gut feeling; you know, the one that told me to run as soon as he entered the store. I would have never experienced that god-awful night." Since then, she has managed to move on successfully with much therapy and guidance from her psychologist, thankfully she lived to tell about it.

That's her story, what about you? What will you live to tell about? Will your story be one that ends in a dismal dismay? Or, will your financial story be of one that promotes triumph, success and intelligence? By following your gut feeling, your internal instincts, your intuition if you will, you will determine which financial story is told about you. Make the right decision and follow your gut feeling; you'll never go wrong, never.

Another indicator is hesitancy. Feeling hesitant about advice from your FA along with a few other negative emotions are all indicators that your FA is messing you over and that he's not being forthright in his dealings with you. Don't ignore those negative feelings, they are there to teach you, to assist you and to even advise you, if you let them. Negative feelings are the complete opposite of feeling confident, assured, convinced, secure and self-sufficient.

Why do I mention this? I mention these emotions, the good and the bad because I want you to understand the difference between the two and what to do should you unfortunately experience the inverse of the good emotions.

Most people are sort of okay with experiencing good emotions as it pertains to the actions of their FA. However, what happens once you begin to experience negative emotions in regards to your FA? How do you successfully manage negative emotions? You don't want to completely destroy the relationship, right? Well, let's continue reading to discover what we should do.

Negative emotions are present to serve as a guide. If you are feeling uneasy about something, look into it, investigate. If there's an agitation or a sincere concern on your part but you don't have any physical evidence that substantiates your feelings, I say put it on the shelf for now but continue to watch closely. Keep your eyes and ears open, and if you are required to make a decision through the lens of scrutiny, err on the side of caution. Remember, the agitation is there for a reason, let it be your guide, your protection, if you will. There's a reason for the feeling, don't ignore it. Consider, whether you've decided if something is actionable or not and you've decided not to act, you've still acted by not acting at all. You've made a decision. A decision is an action. Be confident that you've made the right decision. Trust me, you will soon discover that not acting at all may have quite possibly saved you from financial or relationship ruin; perhaps, it may have even rescued you from both.

If your FA gives you a suggestion, think about it. You don't always have to make a decision to move forward with an FA's suggestion. You can choose to wait. Be patient. One well-known Russian writer stated, "*The two most powerful warriors are patience and time.*" Count Lev Nikolayevich Tolstoy would indeed be correct in his assessment of time and patience. Time does tell the story, in your case, which story will be read on your behalf? Trust the process. Be confident, assured and convinced when you make financial decisions. Don't allow yourself to be pressured into making detrimental decisions. You know, the kind of decisions that tend to benefit someone else and not you? Yeah, those decisions. Don't do that; you're better than that. You can and you will make the right decision because you are going to give a considerable amount of attention to your feelings, the good and the bad ones. Remember, your feelings are there to serve you, now let them.

How do you manage difficult conversations? Have you ever had a thought to speak to someone but then opted not to? Why was that? What made you decide against speaking to that individual? Was it something that they did? Was it something that they said perhaps? What was it? When a person chooses to not speak to another individual, typically, it's for a given reason. We're not talking about overlooking someone and not speaking to them because you didn't see them. We're speaking to the existence of an issue and because of said issue, you decide against speaking to someone for various reasons. Maybe you don't like the way that they make you feel when you're speaking to them.

Perhaps, it's the topic of discussion and not the person themselves that causes you to avoid a direct dissertation. Whatever the reason may be, you don't want to talk about it and definitely not with them. So, how is one to manage such an encounter when the FA is involved? I'm glad that you asked, let's take a gander.

There may be times when you may need to speak with your FA regarding a not-so-happy topic, that's fine; totally understandable. However, the issue is demonstrated when you *regularly* desire to avoid your FA, how does one manage that scenario?

Managing relationships is never an easy task. Relationships require special handling. Personally, I have learned over the years to not be so quick to put a relationship away. Try to work it out, if at all possible.

In relationships, adjustments are sometimes needed. Make every attempt to adjust while trying to see the issue from the other side of the spectrum. However, if all else fails, then go ahead, quietly move on and go your separate ways (quietly, that is).

If the time comes, whereby, you are no longer happy to speak to your FA, there must be a reason. I encourage you to take inventory. Perform a self-check to see why it is that you are feeling sad, depressed, unenthused or perhaps maybe a little angry at the very thought of possibly speaking to your FA. I guarantee, if you are saddened or depressed at the thought of speaking to your FA there's an issue. Perhaps there was a financial transaction made against your better judgment, you allowed the FA to talk you into it, a loss was experienced and now you are very upset. Or, maybe you offered a suggestion to your FA and they displaced your suggestion as though you knew nothing. You were discounted and this made you feel inadequate and embarrassed. After all, who likes feeling inadequate or embarrassed? I know that I don't. Now, because you were made to feel inadequate and embarrassed about *your own assets and decisions,* you've shut down and now refuse to have any type of sound unforced communication with your FA. You're mad. You ask yourself, "Who does he think he is anyway? This is my money! I don't need him!" You know what? You are right! You don't need him to be acting the way that he is towards you in discounting your suggestions. You are also correct in that, it *is* your assets, this is your money and actually, you do not need him, not in this way.

Look, life is hard enough without having to deal with the unsolicited lack of professionalism that some FA's can exude when it comes to their clients. Sometimes, FA's will put you down and make you feel like you don't know what you're talking about because it challenges them. They're insecure and need to boost their confidence, and unfortunately, their confidence may come at the expense of yours. An informed client can prove to be a threat to some FA's. Reason being, when the client is informed, it causes the FA to be on his p's and q's. Every "i" must be dotted and every "t" must be crossed because if it isn't, the informed client will know. An informed client causes the FA to regularly give an account of their actions, decisions and behaviors. So, no, the bad FA doesn't want you to feel empowered to make well-informed decisions. The FA that doesn't want an informed intelligent client is the FA that you want to run far away from. He doesn't have your best interest in mind. You should never want an FA managing your financials that does not have your best interest in mind. As one great man, Albert Einstein, stated, "*Whoever is careless with the truth in small matters cannot be trusted with important matters.*" Just remember, when managing your financials with your FA, if it looks like a mess, sounds like a mess and feels like a mess...guess what it is? Yelp, you've guessed right...it's a mess! Be a prudent, intelligent and well-informed client. The FA that respects those qualities will respect your money; in turn, will respect you. After all, mutual respect is essential for shared success. It's your money, don't ask for respect, demand it.

BROKE BOB

They're broke...so educate yourself.

At some institutions, Financial Advisors (FA) start out making a meager $35K to $40K for the first three years of their FA training. Now, $35K isn't that bad if you're a teenager with no responsibilities or financial obligations and you are still living at home with your parents, but for most FA's, they tend to be adults and so therein lies the problem.

When you are dealing with a broke FA, they think in the direction of only one thing...money. Now, none of us do what we do for free unless we are doing charity work and FA's didn't sign up to do charity work, so I get it, I do; FA's signed up to learn a new skill and to make money. However, with that being said, the very fiber of who they are becomes laced with the thought of making money. They are preoccupied with making money, so much so that at times, instead of a pure conscience leading the way, they allow for money to guide the way. I don't know about you, but I would not want the decision to buy or sell a stock or investment option based upon the fact of making money *alone*. The decision to manage stock and its options should be based up on a variety of factors and not just solely upon the ability for it to make money. Such factors as stock durability, risk ratios, management stability and diversification should all come into play when making financial considerations. Yes, the bottom line is indeed to make money, to make money for all involved hopefully, but at what risk? And, at whose risk? In other words, one should ask themselves *how* is this money going to be made and is this the best route for me to take in regards to my investment. Once again, we arrive right back to destination education. One must educate themselves regarding their financial portfolio, its conditions and possible considerations. One must thoughtfully consider the financial move that the FA is suggesting to be made. Ask yourself: How will this financial move make my portfolio better in the short term? In the long term? Will this financial move negatively impact other positions within my portfolio? How will said financial move impact other financial capacities that you have with other investment firms/organizations? These all are questions, and more, that must be considered when taking the advice of an FA that is relatively less than five years old in the investment game. Financial clients/investors come in a myriad of different ages, sizes, shapes and colors---just like a box of cereal. It is the responsibility of the newly trained eye of the FA to find the fruits, flakes and nuts within that same box of cereal and capitalize for maximum profit and realized gain. Let's take a quick look at how each of the proposed questions may or may not impact you and the thought process that one should have behind each.

Q&A #1:

Will this financial move negatively impact other positions within my portfolio? You bet your bottom dollar that this financially suggested move will have some sort of impact on the bottom line of your portfolio and it's up to you to determine just what type of impact the move will yield. Let's have a look...

If your FA suggest for you to sell some positions, immediately, you should ask why? Again, remember, we are looking at the mentality of the FA. We are needing to understand their rationale and why it is that they do and suggest what they do and suggest so that you can make an informed and well-educated decision. Asking the question of *why* is definitely within the acceptable range of inquiry. I encourage you to get into the habit of questioning almost everything that your new FA suggests. Let your FA know that your many questions are just for educational purposes, you would like to know and understand the rationale behind such recommendations. If your FA doesn't want you to know what you need to know and they get offended because you are placing a demand on them for accurate and thorough information, then you know immediately that you have a problem. I encourage you to begin to understand the relationship of inquiry and understanding as one relates to the other. If you do not begin to explore and understand the awesome dynamic of these two relational factors, you will begin to lose much more than just a few dollars. No one wants to feel as though they have been taken advantage of and in the light of our topic of discussion, ignorance is not so bliss. Ignorance will cost you. It may cost you a little, it may cost you a lot, but make no mistake about it...it will cost you. You will pay a costly price if you remain in a state of not knowing. You must ask yourself, how much are you willing to

pay to remain ignorant - - -without knowledge? I hope that your answer is a resounding nothing! Let's take a little closer look at the relationship between inquiry and understanding as each respectively relates to the other.
First, let's dissect the word inquiry, to inquire. To inquire means to make an investigation; to seek for information by questioning, to search into. Understanding, on the other hand, means to possess the knowledge and ability to judge a particular situation or subject. Understanding also means to possess the power of comprehending or to comprehend; the capacity to apprehend general relations of particulars, the power to make experience intelligible by applying concepts and categories. In other words, you have the ability and power to make an experience an intelligent experience by applying concepts and categorizing information and ideals; however, you can only apply what it is that you understand. So you see, the relationship between the two, inquiry and understanding, is interdependent upon each other. One is depended upon the other. Without questioning with the intent to know and apply, you will lose the power to control your own situation and financial future while in turn handing that very same power over to a financial novice that's posing as an expert as he is making detrimental decisions with your resources about your present and future. Is this what you really want? To have understanding is to possess power. You will possess the power to make an experience or encounter an intelligent one by comprehending what is really going on and not just paying attention to what the FA is saying but most of all paying close

attention to how he is behaving. How is he responding to the idea that you have questions? Does he appear bothered or flustered? Is he irritated at the amount of questions that you are asking? Does he seem impatient towards you because you are asking a lot of questions? Is he short and brief in his responses towards you and your questions? All of these verbal and non-verbal communication queues one must pay very close attention to if he is to remain in the powerful position of personal financial preeminence. In the human resources industry, when interviewing a potential candidate for an open position, the candidate is exposed to a certain type of interview style, this particular style is called behavioral. It used to be that, almost fifty years ago, human resources would conduct a more traditional interview, whereby, the entire purpose of the interview was based upon just your basic average questions to see how well a person could answer questions. Most questions that were asked with in the traditional job interview included hypothetical, cognitive and personality type questions. The traditional interview also allowed the interviewer to kind of get a feel or a generic understanding of the candidate's mannerisms, what they look like, how they articulated etc. However today, fast forward forty-six years roughly, human resources have now discovered that we can no longer just go on looks, how well a candidate answers our questions and mannerisms. However, we now have to get creative and find out how a proposed candidate might behave in a given workplace situation and that's when the concept of behavioral interviewing was born. The behavioral interviewing style was developed in the 1970's by a cluster of industrial psychologists; the actual concept itself wasn't introduced until shortly thereafter. The entire purpose of behavioral interviewing is to determine how one might act in a given situation in the future. Questions are asked of the candidate's past employment and situations to see how they might respond now in a present workplace situation. The specific mindset behind behavioral interviewing is to predict. The interviewer is thinking, "You tell me how you responded in the past, I can then predict how you will respond in the future." Behavioral interviewing allows for the candidate to really be open and create the situation by telling a story of how they overcame some workplace obstacle; whereas, the traditional interviewing style didn't allow for this type of candidate expression. Traditional style interviewing was very subjective to that specific interviewer and its questions often provided close-ended scenarios for the candidate. When interviewing a candidate, the candidate should give what's called a "STAR" reply. Some candidates may even give what's called the "SBO" reply, it's the same as the "STAR" reply. When asked a behavioral interview question such as, "Give me an example of a time when you went above and beyond the call of duty", the candidate is expected to give the Situation/Task (S/T), the Action (A)/Behavior (B) and lastly the Result (R)/Outcome (O). In doing so, the interviewer is suppose to be able to evaluate the candidate more easily and more objectively as it pertains to that particular job opening. The interviewer can just look at the situations, the behaviors and the outcomes and determine from there if the candidate is the best fit for the position. Some benefits listed for applying the behavioral style of interviewing are: it helps to determine if a candidate can show that they are able to produce desired results and outcomes; it causes the candidate to recall real life workplace experiences in detail; establishes predictive behavior and it is believed that companies that invest its resources into behavioral style interviewing attracts top candidates and causes that particular employer to eventually become the employer of choice among job seekers.

I said all of that to say this, if human resources is that meticulous about finding the right candidate for a job, how much more should you be very detailed in finding the right FA to manage your life's resources? When a potential job candidate is interviewing for a job, they don't get frustrated at the process of questioning. And let me say this, if they do, that interview won't last much longer because the frustration will clearly show through and the interviewer will cut the interview short. Someone who really wants the job will happily endure the most gruesome interview and they will do it with a smile. So likewise, if an FA really wants your business, they will endure your inquiring questions and they will do it with a smile. Personally, I do not tolerate any attitude from anyone that desires my business. I will take my business elsewhere. We live in America. There are too many other formidable competitors that I can take my business to that will treat me and my money with respect. I encourage you to think the same, be the same and do the same. Ask those tireless questions. Carefully watch the market. Study the behaviors, the words and the results of your FA; in so doing, you will learn a lot. I once heard a good friend say that actions give way to motives and motives give way to intentions. Pay attention. Ask plenty of thought-provoking intention-seeking questions and stay alert; and by all means, stay alert. Most people have worked very hard to achieve the financial results that they have achieved thus far. Some people are sixty, seventy and even eighty years old, let me ask you this, who has the time, the energy and effort to go make another five million dollars plus just because a novice of an FA decided to squander all of your money away through poor decision-making? Most do not have those kind of resources to expend all over again. So yes, ask the questions, watch the behavior and get the results that you desire. And if you have a gut feeling that this just isn't working out for you, if you are uneasy in your spirit about something, don't wait until you see it to believe it. Believe it, don't see it and take your resources elsewhere. Too many people failed their gut feeling and lost it all. Don't be that person. Be smart. Do right by yourself. Trust yourself and by obeying your gut feeling, this is your wealth not theirs...remember that.

Q&A #2:

Will this financial move make my portfolio better in the short term as well as in the long term? And if so, how? Asking yourself this question could very well save your financial life. Why? Well, let me answer your question by presenting another. Would you go on a boat that's set to arrive in the Bahamas if you knew in advance that the boat was going to sink midway to its destination? I should hope not. Likewise, knowing the immediate and the not-so-immediate rate of return of a potential investment is very crucial to the success of your financial portfolio. If certain investors knew that a certain energy-based company would begin to go under within a 12-month period of an article of inquiry having been written and released about the company, more people would have done more sooner or perhaps not even invested in the company at all. Let's take a quick walk down memory lane.

There was a certain energy-based company that begin in the 1980's. The company had merged with another to form the new entity. During this time, the new entity began to experience record breaking profits, new found wealth. Obviously, the merger was a good move. In 2000, the company reached the number 7 spot on the Fortune 500 list of companies, not bad. The company isn't doing bad at all. In less than a year later of making the Fortune 500 coveted list, things begin to unravel.

Below is a list of actions that negatively impacted the organization and ultimately led to its demise:

- February 2001 – Stock priced closed at $75 roughly. Inside of 11 months later, that same year, the price of the company's stock had plummeted a whopping $74 leaving the price of stock at about a meager $0.26.
- Within six months of an inquiry being released the stock priced had decreased dramatically from $75 to $39.
- Within sixty days roughly, the price of the stock had decreased again by $6 bringing the stock down to $33 from its previous high of $39.
- In ten more days, the price of ownership decreases again to $15 from its previous amount of $33.
- By December of that same year the cost of the stock is worth nearly nothing, closing at the awesome grand price of $0.26 per share. Just to be clear, the closing price was in cents not dollars.
- During this time, multiple changes in executive management and administration have taken place an unprecedented amount of times to defray from the inevitable. Heads were going to roll, the only question remaining was, which heads were rolling first.
- Workers were ordered to destroy all documents with the exception of just the basic documents that were

needed to account for financial transaction and history.

- Six senior executives left within the short time span of twelve months – Do we now see how important short term and long term financial forecasting is to one's portfolio?
- It was proven that the company had indeed inflated its income by a substantial amount of $585 million roughly within the last four years.
- "Before its collapse, (the company) marketed electricity and natural gas, delivered energy and other physical commodities, and provided financial and risk management services to customers around the world."
- "Earnings had been overstated by several hundred millions of dollars".
- Shares were, at one point, worth as much as $90 per share roughly.
- Top execs sold their stock prior to the company's downfall.
- Lower-level employees were prohibited from selling their stock as part of a "401k restriction". In which, in turn, caused some to lose their life savings.
- The company filed for Chapter 11 bankruptcy; in which, by the way was the largest bankruptcy in U.S. history at that time. Therefore, causing multiples of

thousands of company employees to have worthless stock in their pension fund.

- A former VP of the company commits suicide, no doubt due to the indiscretions of the company that he was a part of at one time, that's very unfortunate.
- Within the first nine months of one year, the company had an estimated revenue of $137 billion. By the end of the following year, executives were in jail, some committed suicide, others pleaded the fifth amendment so as not to self-incriminate. Additionally, the auditing firm was indicted with obstructing justice by shredding important documents that would have validated the illegal actions of this particular company.

So again, you ask, "Will this financial move make my portfolio better in the short term as well as in the long term? And if so, how?" And to that I say, you tell me. Based upon the information that I have just shared with you about the company listed above, I think that you are now educated well enough to intelligently answer your own question. If not, at this point, I would definitely suggest that you not invest. I would suggest for you to conduct a little more research and verify if the rigorous financial option of investing is the best option for you at this time.

Q&A #3:

Will this financial move impact other financial capacities that you may have with other investment firms/organizations? And if so, how? This is a very good question and the answer is emphatically yes! Most certainly, one financial move could definitely impact other investments that may be held with other organizations.

One may ask how? This is how...most financial institutions follow what's called a trend. As matter of fact, most companies in most industries follow a trend. A trend is a general course of action or tendency; tendency is a common way of behaving or proceeding. Companies within a given industry tend to follow the trend. That is to say, that they go with the flow of whichever way that the industry leader is flowing. For example, if Wal-Mart set's its price for butter at $1.50 per pound then a nearby neighboring store will more than likely do the same. There are several reasons why an organization will follow the trend. One reason is to remain competitive. If I am selling the same product for the same price but I am in closer proximity to the customer, I have a better chance of the customer coming to my store because my price is the same and I am closer. The second reason that an organization may follow the trend of the industry is to be able to forecast the future. Forecasting allows for an organization to prepare itself. An organization may need to prepare for an industry upswing or a down spiral, depending on the noticed trend. There is safety in forecasting, therefore, it is safe to say that trending provides protection for an organization that trends the industry. Lastly, another reason that a company may follow an industry trend is to properly identify the up and coming trend in hopes of becoming the new industry leader. Quite possibly, an organization may be just one innovative step away from becoming the new leader within its industry. Who can make the next best cell phone? Who can provide the latest and the greatest to the customer without losing revenue, oh and by the way, how fast can you do it? Who can provide the best features for the latest electronic device? Who can? Who can? Who can? That's what it's all about, staying on the cutting edge of innovation. Following the industry's trend just might put that next company in position to be the new leader, and oh, what a coveted position! Once a company has moved into first place as an industry leader, they can now set the rules themselves for others to follow. However, they must remain on task, if not, they will run the risk of losing their position which may not be a good look to investors.

There are two reasons why you should closely monitor your investments with all firms that you're working with. The first reason is just as I referred to directly above, trending. If a company follows industry trends, you very well might be invested in the same stock options at your other investment firm. If this is the case, if one stock plummets, so does the same stock at the other organization. You want to make sure that when you establish your financial portfolio that you diversify your investments. To diversify means that you do not have the same stock as your entire stock option with a particular investment firm. For example, let's say that you work at company A. Company A allows for you as an employee to purchase stock. You decide to have your entire 401k pension plan filled with nothing but stock from company A. If company A goes out of business, yes your employer, what are you going to do then? So, you see, the best thing to do is to have a little of this and a little of that to make sure that you don't put all of your eggs in one basket, so to speak. Additionally, to diversify also means to have different types of stock and financial options in many different types of financial instruments. For example, if a person were to diversify in this instance, one might have 20% of their financial investment portfolio stock options in one type of basic stock; and yet, have the remaining 80% of their portfolio invested in a variety of certain types of bonds, long term as well as short term financial instruments. Then, you'll also want to make sure that you have some finances that are liquid for emergency purposes. So you see, clearly, diversifying your portfolio investments is an essential for strategic financial portfolio success.

The second reason to closely monitor your investments with the other firm is so that you can catch any possible major losses *immediately*. If your portfolio begin to bleed cash at one investment firm, you may be able to sell some options at the other institution to cover the loss against your portfolio with the other investment firm. Typically, selling one option to cover the loss in another portfolio is a common practice. One may have several portfolio accounts with one firm. Your portfolios don't necessarily have to be at several other firms in order for you to borrow against them or to sell stock to cover a loss against another stock. There is a software program called OneView. OneView allows your FA to view all of the investments that you have at all other investments firms. You have to enroll, which is basically you giving permission to the FA to view the other investments. The purpose of OneView is to allow your FA to see those other investments that you hold with other companies so that they can figure out how to capitalize and possibly have you move all investments over to the one FA and their company. One should be careful in moving all investments to one company, there are a myriad of options to consider when seriously contemplating such a move. The most important thing that you want to really consider when moving your portfolio from one organization to another, you'll want to consider the source and your gut feeling. If it doesn't feel right, don't do it. Take your time. There is no law against being patient and making calculated and educationally sound moves, even if it means that you make no move at all. You still made a move and that move was in your favor. Always remember to be patient. In review, we did see that, one move at one investment firm can definitely impact your financial capacity to function successfully at another investment firm. In conclusion, portfolio losses may need to be covered, stock options may need to be sold at one investment firm to cover said losses at another; and most of all, do remember to diversify and make sure that you do not have the same stock options in one portfolio that you have in another. Unless of course, being of a sound mind, that is what you are deciding to do; if so, that is perfectly okay, after all, it is your money. Again, just remember to be patient and to continue to make the best financially educated decision that's just right for you.

#1: **Actions** –

The word action means behavior, conduct, a thing that is done or an act of will. To effectively understand your FA, you'll need to know or at least anticipate their actions and you'll be able to do this efficiently if you are able to understand how they think, which goes back to mentality. What is the direct relationship between the mental process and the actionable process of a person? How does the thoughts of a person translate into the behaviors of a person or vice versa? How can I look at the translated thoughts and behavior of my FA and accurately anticipate their next move (calculating their efforts)?

How can I look at the conduct of my FA and understand what my next move should be as the client (calculating my efforts)? To anticipate means to do something before someone else, to foresee and deal with in advance, getting ahead so as to stop or interrupt something in its course (forestall), checking another's intention by acting first and to prevent- taking advance measures against something or someone that is possible or probable. Action is tangible.

What is the direct relationship between the mental process and the actionable process of a person? A process is a series of actions or steps taken in order to achieve a desired end. What a person is thinking will manifest on the outside; conversely, what a person manifests on the outside has just now told you what they were thinking on the inside. The direct correlation between the mental state and the actionable state of a person is the results of that person. While working with your FA, you'll definitely want to pay close attention to what he does because this will tell you how he thinks. No, we cannot read minds but we can read and understand actions, behaviors and conduct.

How does the thoughts of a person translate into behaviors and vice versa? The thoughts of a person translate into behaviors through actions. Translate means to say the same thing just in a different way or language so that a greater understanding can be gained. Your FA is communicating to you through their behavior all of the time. However, you must be keenly adept to understand exactly what is being communicated. In other words, you must pay attention. Either you pay attention or you pay with a possible financial loss; but either way, you will pay. Why not make the decision that is most beneficial to you? I would. I once heard someone say, "When people show you who they are, believe them" and I totally agree with this statement. The operative phrase in the afore mentioned statement is, "When people show you...". Actions do speak louder than words. Your FA may say what they think you want to hear, but watch their actions. Watch the behavior of the FA. Are they "showing" you what you want to see? Are their actions and words aligning themselves or no? Don't be deceived. If it walks like a duck, looks like a duck and quacks like a duck then guess what it is that you just might be looking at? Yelp! You guessed it, a dag on duck! Smart? Yes. Rocket Science? No, not hardly. Just pay attention and watch closely. I guarantee, you and your money will be the better for it...trust and believe.

Behaviors are translators. Behavior is communicating something to the observer all of the time. The question is, for the observer, are they listening? Are they giving attention to what's being communicated through the common activity of behavior. Behavior communicates thoughts. Thoughts cause behavior to be repeated, therefore, yielding repeated behavioral results. Behavior is very important to observed. As a matter of fact, Burrhus Frederic Skinner (aka B.F. Skinner) initiated and devoted an entire discipline of psychology (operant conditioning) to the observant study of behavior. Skinner had such thoughts as: behavior has a direct relationship to the environment that's surrounding it and that behavior drives thoughts. Skinner believed that thoroughly observing the actions and consequences of said actions of a subject was the very best way to understanding the "why" behind the "who". Why do people do what they do? According to Skinner, studying a person's rationale of an action and its consequences would indeed tell all and I would have to agree. There are always exceptions to every rule. However, as mentioned before, actions do speak louder than words. So, again I ask, what is your FA telling you through the communication of observed behavior? Pay attention, listen up, take notes and act responsibly within the best interest of you and your family.

Calculating the FA's next move. How can I look at the translated thoughts and behavior of my FA and accurately anticipate their next move?

Basically, you are wanting to know, how can you remain one step ahead in the game? Great ask! Reason being, if you can accurately calculate, then you can effectively plan ahead to counter any move that might prove to be unfavorable for you. For example, let's take a look at the game of basketball for instance. Basketball is a team sport. On the floor during a game, you have five team members from each team participating and playing in the game. Each player contributes to the game. If you are the offensive team (the team with the ball), each of the five players that are on the floor has a specific role to play in order to reach its short-term goal of scoring a basket; while, always playing with the long-term goal in mind of ultimately winning the game. On an offensive team you have five positions: the point guard (1), the shooting guard (2), small forward (3), power forward (4) and the center (5). Next, we are going to take a look into each of the respective roles of all five positions. Hang tight. I promise you, this will all come together quite beautifully like a full-scale 90 musician orchestra harmoniously playing a symphony. I guarantee, it will all come together majestically, stay tuned.

So, we have these five basketball positions: the 1, 2, 3, 4 and the 5. The one position, the point guard, he runs the floor. He is the general of it all. He tells players where to go. He decides which player gets the ball. He even decides if he wants the ball back from another player. Quite frankly, he's like the quarterback on a football team, he dictates pretty much everything on the basketball floor as it pertains to his teammates. Simply stated, he runs the show, period. With that being said, the coach and his one position absolutely unequivocally must have an amazing relationship as the one carries out the orders of the coach onto the floor. Do you see how disastrous this could be if the one position and the coach didn't get along? If they were not in agreement, on the same page, if you will? Personally, I've seen it done and it's not a pretty sight at all. Typically, point guards are small and quick, however, the position and the people that play the position has emerged into something new over the years. Still keeping in line with the fundamentals of the position but now, a point guard can be 6 feet 6 inches tall or even taller listing a grand size of 6 feet 8 inches tall. The key components that a good point guard must have in today's game is strong leadership skills, great passing skills and the knowledge of knowing how to run a team on the floor, that's it. You don't have to be tall, you don't have to be short. One must, however, possess the above-mentioned characteristics for one to be seriously considered for such a position.

The two. The two position, the shooting guard, is tasked with the awesome responsibility of making outside shots, including three point shots while still possessing great ball handling and leadership skills. The shooting guard, at times, may have to play the point guard position. So, he/she must know how to exemplify most, if not all, of the characteristics of the one when needed. The two is relied upon heavily to score. The shooting guard is just that...a shooter. Often times, the shooting guard is the top scorer on the team because of the position that they play as a shooter/scorer. In order for one to be considered a really good two, he/she must be able to be versatile while playing their role. Being able to do more than one or two things on the court is essential in today's game of basketball. If a person can shoot, score, defend, block and create steals then they are considered to be a very valuable asset to their team. Why? Awesome question! When a player is able to do more than one thing on the court, they are considered to be multi-dimensional. Multi-dimensional players extend the defense of the other team. It causes the defending team to cover more court space and more players, ultimately causing the defending team to tire more quickly. If you know anything about sports, being tired while playing is not necessarily a strength to one's game. The one that is tired the least has the better chance of winning the game because they are able to think more clearly and execute more precisely. So, you see, knowing how to be flexible and versatile can be key in effectively filling certain roles.

The three. The three position, the small forward, his assignment is to function as the two but with a strong defensive presence. This position is very versatile. The three assists the one and the two with their roles as well as get rebounds. The small forward can handle the ball, hit outside shots as well as defend the best player on the opposing team when playing defense. The three is usually pretty quick and lean. The three is typically referred to as one of the "wing" players as he plays alongside the two. Simply put, this type of position fills in whenever and wherever is necessary, he is counted on very heavily to get the job done. Again, knowing how to be flexible and ready to change at any given time is a key-crucial in being effective.

The four position. The four, the power forward, is the most dominant player (supposedly) on the floor. Now, dominance is not always a given for this position, but at least in theory, they are suppose to be dominant. The power forward is tasked with the responsibility of rebounding the ball as well as providing a little bit of scoring in the paint for their team, but the most important factor for the power forward is rebounding. The four can also block shots as well which is a defensive stand. The physical build of the power forward is tall, strong and broad usually. They must focus on clearing out space under the basket to get keep the opposing team from rebounding so that they themselves can retrieve the rebound. Rebounding is an art. There are very few that perform the task of rebounding very well. In order to be a great rebounder you have to have a strategy, know angles and know the probability of a shot. Some notable great rebounders are: Dennis Rodman, Wilt Chamberlain, Bill Russell, Kareem Abdul-Jabbar and Moses Malone. This five guys played the position right. As a matter of fact, they played the four position so well that they are widely considered to be the best rebounders in the history of the National Basketball Association (NBA), they were just that good. Similarly, for you, it is also very important to be considered the best at what you do. Why? I'm glad you asked. Being the best means that you get the best: the best clients as well as the best opportunities. The word *best* means of the highest quality, excellence or standing. The word *best* also means to be most advantageous, suitable or desirable. Doesn't that sound like something or someone of whom you would like to be? Of whom you would want your FA to be? With whom potential and existing clients would want to do business with and continue to do business with? Right! So you see, being given special consideration of being the best is very profitable for not only you but for your clients as well; likewise, for your clients, they will be given the best information, strategies and service when allowing you, *the best*, to serve them.

Lastly, the five. The five position, the Center, is usually the tallest or biggest player on the team. Their role is much like that of the four, with the exception of the fact that they are typically much taller than the four (7 feet and taller) and they are considered to be thee rebounder and thee shot blocker of the team. Although the four position does the same as the five, it's certainly not to the extent and level that the five performs its shot blocking, shooting and rebounding skills, there is a distinct difference between the two. On many teams, the five is considered to be a great asset as he/she serves as the last line of defense regarding the opponent. In times past, if a team didn't have a good dominant center, that team was considered to not be a dominant force, therefore, a formidable opponent at all. Since then, times and the game has changed and teams are now actually able to win games and championships even without a dominant center. Albeit, a team must still have one in place to play said position, a center that is. Being able to dominate one's personal environment is a key element to personal success.

To tie it all in as promised before, you asked, "How can I remain one step ahead in the game?" The reply given for such a question was that if you can accurately calculate, then you can effectively plan ahead to counter any move that might prove to be unfavorable for you. Remember? Good, you remembered. Then we proceeded to learn about the awesome game of basketball, its strategies along with its various positions and roles. We learned that basketball players, if they are going to play the game well, must possess certain skill sets, leadership abilities and aptitudes. We also learned that, if the game is to be played well that the player must also be flexible and versatile so as to cover supplementary roles of players should the need arise. Additionally, we learned about being the best and why the special designation of being the best is profitable for all, for you and for the client alike. Lastly, we were reminded that although skill sets, abilities and information may change, all five roles must be filled on the game floor or the game cannot be played. Learning to dominate your environment is a key essential for learning to dominate your life. Likewise, your FA, they should exemplify most, if not all, of the key elements that were discussed in the basketball game analogy. Your FA should be flexible and versatile in their methods and approach. They should also possess a certain skill set and ability to manage your portfolio without crashing and burning. Finally, your FA should be able to dominate the measurables of each decision; all the while, demonstrating to all who observe that they are indeed the best and should be selected. If you are able to determine, find and locate these characteristics in your FA, then Sir/Madam, you have found yourself one heck of an Advisor and staying ahead of the game as it pertains to them will be the least of your concern. You've found an authentic gem, keep them!

As the client, what should I look for in my FA in determining if they are worth the time or not? Great inquiry! In order to "look" or to observe correctly, you must know what to look for. Knowing what to look for will definitely increase your chances of properly identifying a true issue or even help you to properly identify the correct behavior, thoughts and actions of your FA. You may actually have a good FA believe it or not, but you will never know if you don't know how to properly identify and understand what you're observing. There are four things that you want to look for when properly observing your FA and they are: seem rushed, constant money movement, long response times and poor tone of communication. All of these observations are definite red flags. What we will do in the section is help you to recognize the red flags, understand the inherent meaning of each and provide a strategy for your next move. Sound good? Awesome, let's get started!

Observation#1: Seems rushed. When you speak to your FA and they seem rushed, like they don't really have time to speak with you; then Houston, we have a problem. What this means is that your business no longer matters. When your FA is communicating to you with a long stick, they are basically saying that your business is no longer important to them, simply stated, they do not care. People take time for what matters most. And right now, your business is on the back burner with your FA and is quite unimportant. Now, to the credit of the FA (*partial only*), they may be genuinely too busy and not even know it. They may have too many clients; possibly, they may have themselves spread too thin but haven't realized it. Or, it may be that the FA has a new workload and haven't made the adjustment quite yet. The issue could be a myriad of different things, that's why it's important to ask questions and pay attention so that you can know exactly what it is that you are dealing with.

The strategy of next. As the client, what should my next move be? The next move that you should make would be to investigate. Ask direct questions of your FA. Make them feel uneasy just as you feel uneasy having to now manage such confusion. Personally, when it comes to my money, my FA must ALWAYS have time for me. If they don't have time for me, then they don't have time for my money, PERIOD. Now, I am pretty reasonable with my requests. However, within 24-48 business hours at the most, I must receive a return phone call, text or email with no exceptions. It's not that hard to get back with someone in today's technology world. Especially with all of the various ways and methods of communication, there is absolutely no excuse for your FA to not contact you within a reasonable amount of time. I don't even mind talking to the assistant at times, but if my requests requires the direct and immediate attention of my FA, I'd better get it; and you too, should require the same.

The same amount of energy, time and effort that it took for your FA to get your business, the same is also required to retain your business. The concept is called retention. Your FA must understand the concept of retention or you must move on. Why? To answer that, let me ask you this, if your FA isn't giving you the correct amount of attention, how much direct attention do you think that he's properly giving to your money? Yelp, you guessed right; hardly none, if any at all. So, start planning. Do your research. And if needed, move on.

Observation#2: Constant money movement. When there is constant money movement, this is never good. When money is being moved constantly at an irregular pace, this could mean that your FA is trying to extract extra commission and fees from you. Every time that a financial transaction is completed on your account, a fee or some type of commission is being received by your FA. I encourage you to pay close attention to how many times money your money moves within your portfolio. Also, tally up all of the fees and commission that has been assessed to your portfolio as well. Is this an acceptable amount for you? Is the amount what you pretty much thought that you would pay quarterly or annually? If not, speak up. Again, inquire and investigate what you should and should not be paying in regards to fees and commission; I will admit, this step will require some due diligence on your part. It will require you to read and to study. It may even require you to study the markets a bit just to familiarize yourself with the pattern of certain funds and stocks. However, you should be studying the market anyway since this is your money and not theirs. Never leave the vitality of your wealth in the hands of someone else. Do you really have another forty or fifty years to start all over should your portfolio go belly up? I know that I don't. In fact, most people don't have an extra forty or fifty years just to start all over again simply because they chose to close their eyes and not pay attention. When my kids were growing up, my husband and I allowed no one to watch our kids but us. Every now and again we would permit a select few to watch our kids, however, we could count them on the first three fingers of our left hand. We were always taught that our kids are our responsibility and no one else's. We carried this mentality throughout the entirety of their school-aged years. Our kids were home-schooled with a tuition-based education. My kids never seen the inside of a daycare. When attending church services, we use to allow our children to attend the little kids classes; however, we soon discovered that often times, this too, served as a baby sitting service. Although, a less formal and free service, it was still considered babysitting. More times than not, our kids would come home with colds that they had picked up from other kids that were sick in class. We would then get all four kids healed up and restored back to good health, only to repeat the same cycle of sickness the following week. Again we would have another sick child for yet another week. It was horrible! Finally, we got the message and decided to just keep the kids in the regular church service with the rest of us adults. Things worked out, and we, as well as our kids were the better for it. Was it work? Yes! Did adjustments have to be made? Yes! Were we nervous at first? Yes! Simultaneously, it was very rewarding as well as we did not have to rush to church service any longer to try to get all four kids signed in for class. Additionally, we no longer had to stand in long lines after service waiting to pick up our children; rather, we could just leave right out the door avoiding extra traffic. And the greatest benefit of them all, we no longer had to purchase cold medicine at an unprecedented rate because we had four sick children to try to cure before the next Sunday. It was lovely! More money and more time for us, HOORAY! So, what am I saying? Awesome ask! What I am saying is that your money is your responsibility. Treat your money as though it were your precious little children, children that you wish for no one else to manage but you. Losing a child to negligence is totally unacceptable and the same should hold true as it pertains to your money. Losing money to negligence should never be accepted by you. Just as my husband and I experienced a lot of issues with our kids attending "the church babysitting service", you too, will experience financial issues as well if you are not studious and diligent in watching over your money. When my husband and I took full ownership over the education, recreational and personal development of our children, we had more peace and knew exactly what to expect 98% of the time. There weren't too many things that "surprised" us because we were always in tune and aware when it came to our children; the same should be said of you. You also should do the same with your children which is your money that's in your portfolio. If you have $200 million in your portfolio, then consider yourself as having 200 million children. Every one of those children matter and mustn't be lost due to negligence on behalf of you or the FA. In exercising due diligence over your portfolio, you will avoid so many financial pitfalls and mistakes because you are paying attention. Due to the nature of the market, a little financial loss may occur anyway. However, the goal should always be to lose as less as possible. Throwing money away due to lack of attention should never be acceptable to anyone and most certainly, not to you. Again, most do not have another forty or fifty years to start all over financially; the Great Depression of 1929 taught us that, right? Investors pulled out at an unprecedented rate causing fear and panic and the rest is as we say...history. So please, I encourage you to do your homework and don't let history repeat itself in your own life. Let's do our research and not have our own personal Great Depression, especially when we can avoid it through thorough research and due diligence. You can do it, I know you can! Know, at all times, how much you are paying in fees and commission. Know, at all times, what's in your portfolio and if anything has been moved or sold recently. Always know your numbers. Remember, there's safety in knowing. Knowledge truly is power.

The strategy of next. As the client, what should my next move be? The next move that you should make is to be firm with your FA. If you do not wish to move money, tell him. Be bold but stay professional. No need to end a relationship through unprofessionalism if you don't have to. After all, they do have your money, at least for the time being anyway so keep it professional. Also, continue to watch your monthly statements. A lot of times, clients will disregard the monthly statements and only pay attention to the information when needed. Please pay attention to your statements; that way, if something changes from one month to the next, you're on top of it. Let's pay attention at all times. And again, I encourage you to ask plenty of questions, if needed.

Observation#3: Long response times. When the FA is taking longer than normal to reply to your request via a phone call, text or email know that this is not good business. The standard turn around time for most business replies is within 24-48 business hours. Now, business hours, typically are Monday through Friday excluding all major holidays. However, due to the sensitive nature and time constraints of most financial requests along with the industry and market closure times, time is always of the essence when it comes to the industry and your money. So, your FA should definitely be sensitive to the fact that an almost immediate response is required. Even if the initial response is just an acknowledgement that your request has been received, a timely response should be provided.

The strategy of next. What should my next move be? As the client, if your FA is not responding in a timely manner, your next move should be to address the issue directly with your FA. Why? Reason being, if this negligent behavior continues, it could cost you a lot of money. For example, you may wish to sell or purchase a position before the market closes. Buying low and selling high is a fundamental within the industry. If you miss out on said opportunity because of someone's lackadaisical communications, this is definitely not good. One could stand to lose a lot of money missing an opportunity to buy or sell. In my personal experience, I have seen client's buy and sell for very specific reasons. Perhaps there is a family emergency that calls for a portion of assets to be sold for immediate access to funds. With most trades being T+3 (trade day plus three more days), missing even a simple text can cause one to miss a crucial deadline. So, again, if your FA is not responding to your phone calls, texts, emails etc. within a timely manner, address this issue immediately. In so doing, you could be saving yourself from a lot more trouble down the line. When people show you who they are, believe them. Don't ignore them, believe them!

Observation#4: Poor tone of communication. The word *condescend* means to behave as if one is conscious of descending from a superior position, rank or dignity. Your FA should not be speaking to you as if you are a two-year old, as if he is stooping down to a lower level just to talk to you. You should never be considered as an inconvenience to your FA. Again, your FA should *not* be speaking to you as though you are an infidel and unable to understand basic communications, this type of communication is unprofessional and unnecessary; do not permit it to happen. Always make sure that your FA remain in a professional position with you at all times. For in so doing, you communicate to them what your expectations are, how it is that they should be treating you as well as what their poise and posture should be as it pertains to governing your financial affairs. When your FA is speaking to you in an unprofessional manner, this means that they are disrespecting you. Whether the FA means to or not, in speaking to you in a such a way, they are not showing you any respect. The word respect means to esteem, to honor. Respect also means to bestow a sense of worth or excellence upon a person. When your FA is not communicating to you in a respectful manner, they are not honoring you. To esteem means to appreciate, to favor and to admire. The opposite of esteem is disdain. Disdain means to count unworthy, to consider something beneath oneself. Why am I taking a few extra lines to define simple words that most of us already know the basic definition to? I am taking the time to define because I want to really make sure that you understand the true meaning of such words. With understanding comes responsibility. Now that you *know*, what are you now going to do about it should you make such a discovery? It's up to you to teach people how to treat you. Do not be afraid of your FA. In all honesty, your FA is suppose to be your friend, your comrade, if you will. They are suppose to be showing you the way to the promise land without stealing the promise from you. Granted, it takes a while to get to know people. However, let's not forget that we must, at all times, hold all people accountable for their words as well as their actions. Simultaneously, being disrespected is definitely a breach of relationship that demands that immediate attention be given to such infringement. If you address it now, you won't have to address it later because either you'll move on or they would've corrected their communications to fit the professional criteria of the relationship.

The strategy of next. What should my next move be? As the client, you will want to remain professional at all times, even when the FA does not. Also, you will want to address the issue with a resolution in mind. Should the FA not change their position and style of communication of disrespect, then you must make a decision as to terminate the relationship or to continue there in. It's totally up to you. It's a total decision that is governed by you the client, however, I must warn that should you stay in such a relationship with no change, the bleeding will spread. More than likely, the bleeding will spread over into your financial portfolio because consistent disrespect is a state of mind, it's a mental positioning. Disrespect is not necessarily a behavior alone, but rather it's a behavior that's triggered by a set of pre-existing thoughts that has caused such violation to occur. You are better than that. Do not allow yourself to be disrespected at any time, and *especially* in regards to your financials. Be strong, be educated, be polite; and most of all, be professional. Nonetheless, do manage the process and manage it well. You can do it!

A broke FA might say things like...

- "That's very expensive." – Although this may indeed be true, you as the client should be the deciding factor as to what is and what is not *expensive* for you, this is certainly not the correct call for your FA to make. They can make the statement, but please know, that it's a mindset that will ultimately try to sway you to go their way and not your own. You should always make the final educated decision and you should always write your own checks, period.

- The FA may continue to make references in not taking some educated financial risks. Reason being, they may be motivated by fear and believe that "staying small" will keep you safe. You will always want to go with your gut feeling, as we call it. Remember, this is your money, not the FA's. If you lose it all, it was your decision. Do not allow the fear of others to motivate you. You motivate you and do what's in your heart to do. Make decisions that you can live with comfortably. If you make a mistake because of a decision that you made then you would have learned. Conversely, if you make a mistake and fail because of someone else's decision, then you'll know better next time. Make your own decisions and make your own mistakes, own them. Never allow someone else to make a mistake through you. Take ownership and own your life, in all aspects of the decision; you make it, not them.

My Experience...

My professional experience behind the curtain has been one of many vast experiences. Personally, I'd like to speak to the statement that I made directly above when discussing the five position. I stated, "*Being able to dominate one's personal environment is a key element to personal success.*" In making this statement, I discovered that some clients, not all, are not willing to dominate their personal environment. To dominate means to rule over; govern; control. Too many times, I have witnessed the client just handing over total control and autonomy of their financial position to an FA that could care less about them as a client. I remember speaking to one client regarding their account. They knew absolutely nothing about their account but what their FA told them. When it came time to verify certain positions for certain transactions, they had no clue. The client even had the audacity to get persnickety with me because I was asking things of them that they should have known but didn't know because they relied upon their FA for everything. Answer me this, how can you dominate the financial environment of your life when you know nothing of value as it pertains to your account? You can't. You cannot dominate and ensure personal financial success by handing over most account details to your FA without having checks and balances in place. Who is going to make sure that your FA acts fiscally responsible as it pertains to your account? Additionally, who is going to make sure that your FA communicates any and all managed account transactions along with any possible financial implications for you as the client? Lastly, who is going to make sure that you are being assessed the correct amount of fees? Who is going to ensure that you are not being overcharged or taxed for positions that you took a loss on but was stated that you profited from? The government? I think not. The person that should always govern the FA subsequently after the FA governs themselves is you, the client.

Recourse...

What recourse does the client have against such intangible yet tangible actions, thoughts and behaviors? As the client, you have the option, the alternative and the choice to remedy these kinds of situations and behaviors by paying close attention to what's before you. Pay close attention to what's being spoken. Lastly, pay close attention to what's being done. Pay close attention to your monthly statements, don't just disregard them, be an educated client and actually read them. Learn how to read the data and remember it. Ask thought-provoking and sensible questions, this will keep every one on their toes (including you as the client). Be an active client. Stay actively involved in the process of your account and its transactions. Know what's going on and if you don't know, ask. Staying informed, educated and abreast of the current details of your account is the best recourse and defense that you have against a significant major financial loss. Even if you do take a financial hit, at least you knew that it was coming. Being aware will help you to brace yourself for possible financial impact and it will also help you to soften the blow. At all times, know you; know your financial information and most of all know your Financial Advisor. As you make these significant moves, you will begin to feel more confident and more comfortable regarding your financial position. You are no longer in the dark; rather, you are now fully aware of what's going on and that's a good thing.

TIMMY TOO MANY

They have too many clients.

Too many clients is just that...too many clients. Many times, an FA may pick up client after client in hopes of maintaining financial stability but an abundance of clients does not necessarily guarantee an abundance of revenue. Strategy is key when working with clients. Moreover, a successful client service strategy is essential to the sustained success of any Financial Advisor. Once a client is obtained, they must also be retained; and it's that part, the retention part, that can get a little tricky for the FA. Let's have a look.

Retaining a substantial client base can prove to be quite problematic for the FA because of several reasons. The first reason is that, the client themselves may not fully understand the business processes that are implemented, however required, when managing the client-advisor stratum. Secondly, the FA may not realize the level of client base that he has methodically acquired, its expectations along with its requirements. The FA may not even realize the amount of deliberate effort and resolve that he will need to demonstrate within himself so that he may successfully maintain said client base. All of the above mentions must be earnestly and thoroughly considered if the FA is going to effectively manage a highly quantitative client base.

As a client, what does this mean to you? One may ask, "Why wouldn't my Financial Advisor want me to know that he has too many clients? Isn't an abundance of clients a sign of a successful and profitable Financial Advisor?" Those are very good questions. However, let me provide you with some insight as to how the FA actually thinks when it comes to how the client may perceive such an extensive client base.

Bill Gates stated, "*The outside perception and inside perception of Microsoft are so different.*" What Mr. Gates is simply stating is that how one perceives the same organism totally depends upon the position of each perspective. One person may view the company as one way based upon their internal view; while simultaneously, another individual may view the very same company from a totally different perspective solely predicated upon the vantage point of that particular assessor, which is outside of the company.

Why wouldn't the FA want their client to know that that they have too many clients? An FA may not want their client to be aware to the fact that they may have too many clients because it may not be perceived too well; again, depending on who's looking through the glass. Basically, it may not be the best look for the FA. One may construe the busyness of clients as an overworked Financial Advisor. An overworked FA could prove to be a bad FA. How so? It may prove to cause a lack of attention to detail. An overworked FA could quite possibly be placed into a mistaken position to impose a bad financial decision. As we all know, bad financial decisions typically do not produce good financial results. Especially when bad financial decisions include the personal finances of said individual, aka the client.

I distinctively recall one advisor who could not manage the sudden influx of clients. This particular advisor started out with a very good sound and manageable client base. Due to the sound technique and practices of the advisor, their existing clients began to refer additional clients their way. The FA was very happy and elated at the sudden increase of the client base. With the growth of its clients also came the growth of client issues; more affectionately known as problems. The FA no longer was able to successfully manage their clients due to less time being available per capita. Decisions were made in a hurry. Less time was applied in building and maintaining client relationships. Soon enough, clients began to take notice and the FA began to notice as well. The end result was a significant loss of 45% of the FA's client base, a bad reputation and an outlook of failure resulting on behalf of the advisor. Eventually, the advisor was able to rebuild again. However, this time, the FA took their time to build strategically and at a pace that proved client efficacy along with a sustained level of success. Be mindful of how you build, always.

An additional reason that an FA may not wish for you to know that they have too many clients is because of the perceived perception; that you the client, just might leave their firm. I mean really, who wants to be looked at as just a number? I know that I don't. Especially when it comes to my money, I *definitely* do not wish to be just a number in a client book. Let's look at this perception a little closer.

Proper portfolio management is key in order for a financial portfolio to be considered successful, profitable, that is. If your FA has too many clients, how will they know exactly how your portfolio is performing? How will they meticulously keep abreast of the gains and losses of your portfolio? How will they continue to offer value added incentives and services? The answer is that they can't. An FA cannot know and manage what they do not to know to manage. Stephen Covey states, "*Management is efficiency...*" If Covey is right, and I believe him to be, then when funds are misappropriated, clients undermanaged while gains and losses are skewed then efficiency is at a loss. A good FA will admit when they can't keep up and quickly make the necessary adjustments. Whether those adjustments cause the FA to move some clients over to a different FA; or by chance, perhaps, the FA elects to create a waiting list and refuse to take on any additional clients, something must be done. The FA must superintend this issue to a manageable resolution or it could damage his firm's reputation by causing further financial impairments for both he and the client. History advises of an FA based in California. This particular FA decided to continue to take on additional clients as well as client-referrals. The additions, seemingly, never ended. Until one day, the additions ended on its own. Clients were lost, reputations destroyed and trust relinquished. It was really a bad deal for all. Dr. John Maxwell says this about a leader, "*A leader is one who knows the way, goes the way, and shows the way.*" Unfortunately, this FA knew neither.

Having too many clients may be kept further hidden by your FA because you might believe that he is making too much money. Believe it or not, some clients are pretty concerned about how much money in commission that their

FA makes. Some clients feel as though, if an FA garners too much money, it may cause greed to set in and then the FA will begin to respond to the influx of clients financially unethically. It's been stated that it is better to have less clients with a higher net-worth versus a lot of clients with a lower-to-average net-worth. One advisor stated, "I decided that it wasn't possible to add value to that many clients, and so now I serve 19 high-net-worth clients." He further added, "It's freeing and I recommend it." Honesty is always the best policy. Even if honesty hurts, be honest. In so doing, the client will know just what to expect and can therefore plan their future based upon truth rather than a fictitious scenario that may prove to be of a grave disservice and disadvantage for all.

One may ask, "What's wrong with a Financial Advisor having an abundance of clients?" As mentioned directly above, having too many clients may negatively impact the servicing aspect of the FA to the client. The client, intentionally possesses a high level of expectation and professionalism of their FA, as they should. However, let me ask you a question, what drastically happens if the FA is not able to deliver what's inherently understood and expected by the client? What impactful scenarios might occur if the client's expectations are not met as intended? What type of disparaging's might eventuate? Yelp, you guessed right, all of the above.

When clients are disappointed, they talk. Clients talk loud and they talk fast; they talk to many and they talk to be heard. With social media as instrumental as it is in today's culture, one social media posting can either make or break a firm. You want an FA that is going to be sensitive to your financial needs and even to some personal ones; if the FA has an abundance of clients, this is rarely going to be the case. I encourage you to choose, but choose wisely. Watch, but watch diligently. Just because an FA *was* a good FA doesn't mean that they automatically *remain* a good FA. Muriel Spark says, "*Be on the alert to recognize...*" and I agree. Stay conscious and alert. Always place a professional demand on your FA to verify how they will respond. It's imperative that you remain in a position of financial control, even if they are the FA, it's your money. Remember that!

Lost time and resources is another detriment of just becoming a number to an FA because their client base is too expansive. Due to overcrowding by some FA's, the client is left to extensive waiting for servicing. While waiting, the client may be losing out on multiple financial opportunities, which in turn, may cause the client to lose out on resourceful opportunities as well. You say how? Sure, let me demonstrate.

I'm going to keep it simple. Let's take, for example, your money. Money is a resource, wouldn't you agree? If your money is at a loss, then your resources are also at a loss. Illustratively, you have $100,000 as your principal balance in your portfolio account. However, due to excessive waiting caused by your FA, you have now lost the distinct opportunity to invest that same $100,000. Now, you have no return on investment because no investment made. Rather, the money was just sitting, or shall we say *waiting*? In turn, you are still left with just the principal balance of $100,000 with no interest gained. No interest gained means that there is no *extra* to put towards resources. Resources are simply the means to produce; the cumulative efforts of one's ability to produce a supply when needed. If you just happened to need some *extra* over and above your initial principal, but you weren't able to realize any gain because the principal amount was never invested, wouldn't this be a loss of a resourceful opportunity? Yes indeed, if I should say so myself. So you see, loss time equals loss resources, which is money, that happens to be a resource. It's all interconnected. Don't allow yourself to become just a number, make the FA work to retain your business. You're worth it.

Growth is an important characteristic to any living organism. An organism is a form of life composed of mutually interdependent parts that maintain various vital processes. Receiving a return on your investment is a process. No, correction, it is a *vital* process. James Cash Penney(JC Penney) says, "*Growth is never by mere chance; it is the result of forces working together.*" In order for your financial portfolio to grow, all parts must be working together as one cohesive unit with an understanding. So, that means that the FA must be working with you and you with the FA and the two of you must both be working for the overall betterment of the portfolio if true increase is to be realized. Any time that something is not growing, it is dying. Impaired growth is a detriment for all contributors. What are you contributing?

Having too many clients, for a Financial Advisor, may actually prove favorable for the FA. A sustained income, perceived success as well as servicing the masses are all viable reasons as to why an FA would prefer to have an abundance of clients.

Sustained income is very important to most people as the amount of lucrative income determines the quality of life that one will live. For most, having money deposited into their bank account is very important. Money allows for Maslow's hierarchy of needs to be consistently met on a regular basis. Typically, breathing, food, water and sleep are preferable for most descent intellectually stimulated individuals. Without a sustained income, breathing, eating, sleeping and proper water ingestion can all be inhibited in an undesirable way. The great Warren Buffet stated, "*Rule No.1: Never lose money. Rule No.2: Never forget rule No.1.*" and I must say that I totally concur. To an FA, losing clients equates to losing money. Sustaining the client base is sustaining income, the two are one and the same.

A key indicator of seeming success is the perceived accumulation of clients. When an FA is perceived to possess a certain amount of clients by others, it then becomes a perceived success. Whether or not an FA is actually successful as it pertains to their financials, remains to be seen. However, as they say, perception is everything and in this game of financial overkill, perception is about the *only* thing that one has to sell initially. To perceive means to become aware of, know, or identify by means of the senses. Robert Delaunay said, "*Our understanding is correlative to our perception.*" The information that we understand through the five senses will determine exactly how we perceive, what we perceive and what we choose to understand as it relates to those perceived perceptions. Simply put, if an FA is perceived to be successful then he is, period.

Let's be clear, success is more than a financial status. Although status is inclusive, it is not however, exclusive to success. Zig Ziglar stated, "*Success must never be measured by how much money you have.*" Success is an environment. The environment of success is comprised of many different pieces. Success is multidimensional, not one dimensional.

Within the environment of success, there should be multiple phases that are present: spiritual, relational, physical, mental and financial. Additionally, there may be other phases that are specific to one individual that may not be applicable to another. Success simply means the prosperous or favorable accomplishment of one's goals. We should always be working to attain positive goals in every area of our lives. As a Financial Advisor, to be truly successful, one should have an equitable amount of each phase that's noticeably visible to all; yet, intrinsically intimate and exclusionary on a personal level.

Well, how should one determine if they have arrived at the desired level of success? Great ask! An FA, specifically, will determine if they have reached that highly desirable level by reviewing their personal goals and objectives that they have set forth for themselves before beginning the journey.

Only the FA themselves can determine if they are successful or not. Now, again, the FA may have a certain level of perceived public success; however, is the FA truly successful? Only the FA can answer this question.

A great place for an FA to review in order for them to ascertain the authenticity of their realized success is in the relationships of their clients. What goals or objectives has the FA established and accomplished in regards to client relationships? Honestly, have those goals been met? Once the FA takes an in-depth review of their respective goals and objectives for each client, the FA will then be able to accurately determine the true level of their actualized, not perceived, success.

Servicing as many clients as possible is another way to appear successful to others, but are you really? There's certainly nothing wrong with servicing as many clients as you can; yet in still, I encourage you to take a look at how it is that those clients are being serviced? As an FA, are you feeling overwhelmed? Are you feeling crowded? Disorganized? Feeling like it all is just a bit too much? If so, then you are servicing beyond your reach. Generally speaking, we typically like to help as many people as we can, this makes us feel good that people are being helped. However, if we are not helping people in the best way possible by being efficient, then we have failed them.

Recently, there was a major investment firm that was fined millions of dollars by the Securities Exchange Commission (SEC) because they were not able to properly manage the servicing of their client base efficiently. Their systems were out dated, thus, the systems of this great investment firm were not charging the client accurately. The firm never caught the mistake and when they were audited, they were found to have been negligent in the servicing of their clients. The investment firm was ordered to pay the clients back all of the monies that were owed them *plus* the firm had to pay a hefty fine worth millions of dollars to the SEC for not paying attention and being negligent in the servicing of their clients through a failed servicing system. This is a perfect example of negligence in client servicing.

After the audit of the investment firm's systems and client files, the firm decided to update their servicing systems to protect against future servicing negligence. Question, why didn't the firm update their systems prior to the findings? Testimony proved that the firm knew that the systems needed replacing but they chose not to replace the failed systems in hopes of saving money. Well, it looks like they will have to wait quite awhile to recoup the money that they had to pay back to impacted clients as well as the money that they had to pay out to the SEC in fines. Due diligence says, "Replace the systems now so as to avoid any possible regulatory and client fees in the future". Douglas Adams once stated, "*To give real service you must add something which cannot be bought or measured with money, and that is sincerity and integrity.*" I must agree with Adams. Integrity is the key to servicing clients successfully.

In the aforementioned scenario, if the investment firm would have demonstrated integrity in this situation, they would have updated the systems in order to avoid such mishaps. Now, because of the findings, I guarantee that the firm ended up paying out more money in fees and fines versus the amount that they would have paid to just update the system. One of the definitions for the word integrity is *unimpaired.* The opposite of the word unimpaired is *impaired.* Impaired means weak, damaged, inadequate, incompetent and deficient in function or performance. Clearly, according to SEC standards, the systems of the firm were deficient and inadequate in providing accurate pricing and servicing for the clients, hence the millions of dollars assessed in fees and fines. Ensuring that integrity is present in servicing the client in all aspects will do nothing but contribute positively to the overall success of an FA's performance with their client as well as with their firm.

The Final

The eventual and conclusive takeaway from this read is to educate yourself, know more about you than they do and to never allow yourself to be taken advantage of through ignorance. As you remain educated about your financials and its status, it will be very challenging for anyone to get over on you. Even if they try, you'll see it coming from a mile away and you'll know how to effectively manage each situation.

When it comes to your finances, ignorance is never bliss and what you don't know *will* hurt you, it may even kill you. Again, who has another forty to fifty years to accumulate wealth all over again? Most people do not have another four decades to amass another level of wealth. Exacting due diligence against the fragility of financial failure is a must. Closing your eyes while driving has never been a smart thing to do. An investment in knowledge pays the best interest (*Benjamin Franklin)*, dividends anyone?

www.ingramcontent.com/pod-product-compliance
Lightning Source LLC
LaVergne TN
LVHW090428210926
848480LV00002B/742
* 9 7 9 8 3 4 9 3 2 8 7 2 5 *